2-23-77

BELTS
FOR
ALL
OCCASIONS

Sarah Hobson

Mills & Boon Limited
London

This book is for Kitty, whose skills taught us so much, from Carol and myself, who shared the experience of belts.

My thanks to Peter Carapetian for his generosity in taking the photographs.

First published in Great Britain 1975 by Mills & Boon Limited, 17–19 Foley Street, London W1A 1DR.

ISBN 0 263 05599 X

Made and Printed in Great Britain by THOMSON LITHO LIMITED, EAST KILBRIDE, SCOTLAND.

Contents

	page
Aspects of the belt	5
Why make one?	9
Materials	10
Equipment	17
Working methods	19
Ribbon belts	25
Variations	28
Turned belts	32
Variations	36
Wide belts, covered buckles	40
Variations	46
Covered buttons	49
More ideas	52
Index	64

Suppliers

Tools Most can be bought in hardware stores or haberdashery departments. In case of difficulty with the clicker's knife, metal straight edge, paring knife and drive punch, try

> Buck & Ryan Ltd
> 101 Tottemham Court Road, London W1

Interlinings Try haberdashery departments, and Woolworths for heavy adhesive tape

Foam rubber Thin sheets from Woolworths; thicker pieces from foam rubber offcut shops

Fabrics Department stores or furnishing shops

Leathers Some craft shops carry leather, or try your nearest tanner—use the classified directory under 'Art & Craft', and 'Leather Manufacturers', but ring first to ask if you can buy single skins. The following are very good:

Light Leather Co. Ltd (for Persian and Domestic leathers, skiver, snakeskin, pigskin) Alpha House, The Hyde, London NW9

Alma (London) Ltd (for heavier skins, especially domestic, and skiver) 18 Clerkenwell Road, London EC1

Prime Leathers Ltd, 30 Tottenham Street, London W1, has a large selection of single skins at cheap prices.

Connolly Bros. Ltd., 39 Charlton Street, London NW1, has cowhide and suede.

Outside London, Harrold Leathers of Bedford stock calf, kid and hide; Gibbs Bros, 72 Overstone Road, Northampton, stock Domestic and oddments.

Glues Most hardware stores and stationers carry a good selection. There are, among others, Copydex (white rubber solution), UHU and Bostik (clear glues), Evo-Stik Impact (brown petroleum adhesive), and Araldite (resin and hardener).

Aspects of the belt

Two hundred diamonds, one huge emerald, and a band of solid gold formed the coronation belt of the present Shah of Iran; impressive certainly, but also functional, for it carried his sword as a symbol of authority. Indeed, metal belts were worn by fighting men in Iran some three thousand years ago.

Throughout its history the belt has been used to carry weapons—sling, dagger, sword and tomahawk. Even today the soldier's uniform has a belt for carrying ammunition or a gun. The belt in battle has been leather buckled with silver, a sash knotted behind, a girdle tying the tunics of Greek and Roman soldiers to allow freedom of movement, and a band of bronze backed with leather and tied in front with a thong. In battle, the belt has also carried the standard to victory or defeat.

Frequently jewels and precious stones adorned the belt as protection against the enemy: amber averted the evil eye, the sapphire prevented captivity, the emerald brought happiness and triumph over sin. The amethyst particularly was a fighting man's jewel, for its influence was believed to help parry weapons.

Provincial Roman buckle in gilt bronze set with garnets, sixth century A.D. *(Victoria & Albert Museum)*

Left: brass rubbing of Sir J. D'Aubernoun, A.D. 1277, Stoke D'Abernon, Surrey. The hip-belt is typical of the Crusades period, when sword and lance were the main weapons. The waist girdle restricted the surcoat and, according to superstition, protected the wearer. The Muslim 'infidel' at this time tucked a dagger into the cloth that bound his waist. (Victoria & Albert Museum: Catalogue of Rubbings of Brasses and Incised Slabs, London, 1972)

Right: Amazon clothed in leopard skin with studded leather belt, taken from a Greek vase. Women seem to wear heavy leather belts only in times of their militancy.

Since it provided the means to victory, the belt assumed symbolic powers: the Mongols sealed alliances by exchanging plundered belts, and the Franks believed that a man took on his enemy's power once he had seized his belt.

For many centuries the belt has served two main functions, decoration and utility. Some are one and not the other, some are a mixture of both. In the Middle Ages a peasant's belt was a strip of raw leather that carried his working tools; in the fifteenth century a collector of rents hung pen and ink from his girdle; the jailer used his belt to carry his keys; the courier, his message bag; the poacher, his game bag; and women, their purses and fans. Now most of these things are carried in pockets or handbags, so that the shape and size of the belt is more decorative than utilitarian, and more determined by fashion than necessity.

The utility of the belt: left, peasant ploughing a field, about 1335–40. The tool hanging from his belt is probably a whetstone for sharpening the coulter. (The Trustees of the British Museum; Luttrell Psalter, MS 42130, f.202v)

Right: combining practicality with the height of fashion, the French courtier carries a fur handmuff on his belt. (Engraving by Bonnart, about 1695; Bibliothèque Nationale, Paris)

Even more than fashion, the availability of materials such as metal, cloth and leather has controlled the development of the belt. When silks and brocades came from China on the Great Trade

Route, only the rich could afford them; with the Industrial Revolution, woven cloth became the fabric of the middle classes. In pastoral England leather was part of everyday life, being used for clothes, vessels, furniture; today it is a luxury. Thus a belt could indicate the status and wealth of its wearer. Tutankhamun's belt was rich with gold and precious stones; his attendants wore unadorned cloth. A German noblewoman of the sixteenth century (see page 30) wore rich brocade beneath her jewelled bodice; her servant probably tied an apron round instead.

The function of the belt in fashion: left, Cretan goddess, about 1600 B.C. A metal belt was probably worn from childhood to constrict the waist. (Heraklion Archaeological Museum. Photo Hirmer Fotoarchiv, Munich)

Right: Victorian lady, 1894 fashion plate. The belt covers the juncture of blouse and skirt; the narrow waist meant a boned corset. (City of Manchester Art Galleries)

Why make one?

The first belt I made was a strip of hessian (burlap) attached in front to a flat wooden butter dish in which I punctured patterns with brass studs. It looked like a Nordic fighting belt and was too uncomfortable to wear. Yet it expressed something in me, and gave me my first conscious contact with making.

What is making? For me it is the experience and exploration of materials, their textures and colours, which can be moulded into shapes that are both functional and decorative. This exploration and experience lead to a knowledge of the medium where control and free expression can be united, and this in turn gives me great satisfaction. I find it satisfying to handle a piece of suede and turn it into a belt, to express an idea with a piece of leather to its advantage and mine, and I am happy that I can wear the finished belt.

There should be no fear in making something, even if it is the first attempt. Fear inhibits a person's expression, and tells him he cannot do it. But each person can do it in his own way to suit his own character. The belt may be decorative, it may be functional, or it may be a combination of both; it will certainly be individual. With luck, it will stimulate enthusiasm and a sense of caring, so that something that is useful also becomes beautiful.

Perhaps that is reason enough for making a belt; the satisfaction, the fun, the utility. There are practical reasons as well, especially economic ones. Making a belt does not require any expensive equipment, nor hours of practice on technical details. A different belt can renew the life of clothes with flamboyance or subtlety; a home-made belt removes the stress of trying to buy what you want; and in hard cash terms, it is cheaper to make one than to buy one.

Materials

The choice of materials bewilders me. I sometimes feel that I can make a belt from anything, but when this happens I rarely succeed. Only when I reduce the possibilities and concentrate on fabric, or colour, or texture, does an idea evolve, and only then can I explore it to full satisfaction. There are two main types of belt: *(1)* fabric or skin cut into a strip, turned onto an interlining and backed; *(2)* skin cut into a strip and stitched or glued raw-edge to a backing. The turned belt allows greater variation, but materials and equipment usually dictate the choice of method.

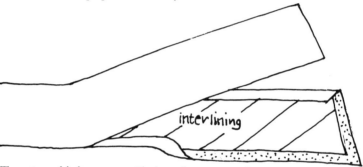

Top: turned belt, reverse side (see also pp 32–35)
Bottom: raw-edge, right side (see also pp 52–54)

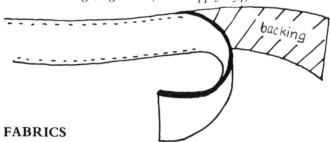

FABRICS

These include the natural fabrics wool, cotton, linen, silk, and the man-made fabrics rayon, nylon, dacron. Fabric is comparatively cheap. It provides a huge range of colours and textures, and is readily available. It is easy to match with clothes, but its fraying properties limit design. It is used almost entirely on turned belts, although a fabric such as felt may be used raw-edge.

LEATHERS

Though more expensive than cloth, I find leather more satisfying to work: it is supple, strong and constantly alive in texture; it is fluid, flexible, yet full of its own character.

The term 'leather' is used for both leather and suede, though they differ to the sight and touch. Leather is tanned, dyed and finished so that the grain, or outer hair side of the skin, is smooth and often shiny (called patent when very glossy). Suede is buffed to a velvety surface on the flesh, the inner side of the skin. Sometimes the reverse side of leather can be used as suede, and, if ironed, vice-versa. Leather, particularly Persian leather, wears well. Suede is less durable and the colours are not always fast.

Turned belts

Skins vary in size and weight, but the following are best for turned belts.

Persian leather and suede is the finest quality sheepskin available, so-called when it was first imported from India through the Persian Gulf. The skins are small, 4–7 sq. ft (37–65 sq. cm), but are finely grained and very supple. Good selection of colours; ideal for turned belts, though more expensive than other types.

Domestic leather and suede is also from sheep, but coarser than Persian leather and, therefore, less easy to work. Comes mainly from New Zealand and Australia. Useful size, 6–9 sq. ft (56–84 sq. cm), and a wide range of colours.

Pigskin split suede turns well, but the quality is not always good. Size: 6–10 sq. ft (56–93 sq. cm); interesting texture and colours.

Calfskin leather and suede skins are larger, 12–15 sq. ft (111–114 sq. cm), and heavier than the others, and have a marvellous grain. Stiff to work, but good for strong belts in simple designs. Subtle colours and finish.

The following are more difficult to find.

Goatskin leather and suede skins are small and often too thick for intricate work, but have an attractive grain.

Kid leather and suede is used mainly for shoes. These very small skins have a soft grain.

Chamois suede was originally antelope skin, but is now lightweight sheepskin and goatskin. It tears easily, but it's cheap. Available in natural cream colour, and sometimes in dyed, washable skins.

Raw-edge belts

Calfskins or hides are best, though the hides are costly because of their size, and more equipment is needed for working because of their weight.

Cowhide leather is heavy and stiff. Needs hand stitching or a leather machine. Size: 18–25 sq. ft (167–232 sq. cm).

Split cowhide suede is more supple than the leather, but heavy. Size: 8–14 sq. ft (74–130 sq. cm). Range of colours.

Pigskin leather has an interesting texture, but is hard to find. Few colours. Size: 6–10 sq. ft (56–93 sq. cm).

PURCHASING LEATHER

It is sometimes difficult to buy single skins because tanners work in hundreds. They may sell you their surplus direct; if not, try craft and leather retail shops.

Try to avoid a fixed idea of your needs, but see and feel which skins inspire you. The weight, texture, and size will probably determine the style of the belt.

Leather is sold by the skin, though large hides are sometimes sold by the half or quarter. Prices are quoted per square foot: sizes are marked on the back of each skin, with $\frac{1}{4}$, $\frac{1}{2}$, $\frac{3}{4}$ represented by ^{1}, ^{2}, ^{3}, respectively. A skin marked 6^2 costs $6\frac{1}{2}$ times the square foot price.

Don't be deterred by difficulties. You will need to explore and accumulate experience, for leather has many forms and finishes, according to the manufacturer.

If possible, check the skin before buying: too many blemishes mean heavy wastage. And if you are not very good at mathematics, ask for the cost of the whole skin before the bill is written.

REPTILE SKINS

Bright colours, exciting textures, minimum wastage: these skins are thin but tough, and easy to work. Good size for a single belt: 4″–8″ (10–20 cm) wide, 2–4 ft (60–120 cm) long. Use raw-edge with stiff backing and interlining, or turned onto firm interlining. Excellent for covering buckles.

Watersnake, whipsnake, python and cobra are not threatened by extinction.

Reptile skins are difficult to find, but are stocked by some leather merchants.

PLASTICS AND PVC

Though fabric-backed, they do not fray, and can be fun, shiny, bright. They are good for experiment and ephemeral moods, though difficult to work, as they do not glue well. Use lightweight for turned belts.

IMITATION LEATHERS

It is often cheaper and less trouble to buy plastic 'leather' and fabric 'suede'. But they never smell like the real thing, or have the richness, texture, and suppleness, which for me are pleasurable —I should say essential—properties. They are also difficult to work.

OTHER MATERIALS

I have not included wood or metal because they require specific skills. Nor have I mentioned unusual materials, for only the maker can find and adapt them to suit his imagination. Not everyone likes a belt of newspaper stitched between polythene where the Bishop of London's head lies beside Tonight's Menu.

STORAGE

Fold or roll fabrics right side in. Store in a drawer or box away from dust.

Roll plastics right side out. Dust can easily be wiped off.

Never fold skins, for the crease marks remain. Roll from head to tail with the grain side out to prevent wrinkles. Roll spare pieces in with the skin from which they were cut. Snakeskins tend to spring loose, so tie them gently with a piece of string.

Store on shelves or in a long drawer; skins keep for years, but their colours will fade in direct light.

For more information on leathers, see J. W. Waterer: *Leather Craftsmanship*, G. Bell, London, 1968, and X. L. Parker: *Working with leather*, Pitman, London, 1973.

BACKING

All turned and most raw-edge belts need backing to seal loose ends and prevent friction against clothes. The best is skiver, a specially prepared, almost paper-thin leather that sticks effectively. Though it is not supple, it can easily be trimmed to difficult shapes. Size: 6–11 sq. ft (56–102 sq. cm). Stocked by most retail leather shops.

Otherwise, use any material that is thin and does not fray, such as fabric-backed lightweight plastic. Use cheap leather or offcuts for backing flimsy raw-edge belts.

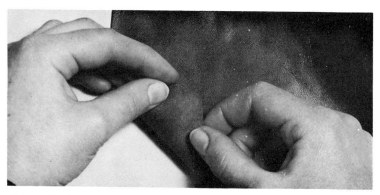

Skiver for backing belts, showing front and reverse. It tears easily if inadequately stuck. It gives little support to flimsy materials, but is essential for turned belts.

INTERLININGS

Most turned and some raw-edge belts need an interlining (preferably adhesive on one side); any strip of material works that is straight-edged and firm.

Adhesive tape is ironed on. Use the heavier types that are made for carpets and heavy fabrics. Normally in widths of 3″ (7.5 cm), 2″ (5 cm), 1½″ (4 cm).

Belt backing is non-adhesive, but comes in several widths. Use the smooth, unridged side against the material.

Waistband interlining is sometimes adhesive, but is often too flimsy for use. Petersham is firmer, but its ribbed surface shows through lighter materials, including leathers.

A selection of interlinings for turned belts, and for raw-edge belts that need strengthening

ADHESIVES

Experiment with glues to see which suits a particular material. Most adhere only to their own type and drying time varies. The following adhesives allow adjustment when bringing the two surfaces together, provided it is done quickly.

Gluing equipment: thin foam rubber tied into a bundle, and thick foam rubber, both for spreading rubber solution; rubber solution ready for use in a bowl; brown glue, with used paintbrush soaking in white spirit. Replace the foam rubber whenever the surface is hard from dried rubber solution.

White rubber solution is good for skins and fabrics, especially over large areas. Does not bind shiny surfaces, so sandpaper leather and snakeskin. Apply with foam rubber on two surfaces and stick together when semi-transparent.

Clear adhesive is useful on absorbent fabrics, plastics, and for difficult turnings. Apply to one surface only and stick immediately.

Brown petroleum mixture bonds shiny surfaces, including metal and patent. Use for points of stress that need strong binding. Apply with paintbrush on two surfaces.

Resin and hardener mixture is occasionally useful for foolproof binding on metal. Apply with spatula on one surface. Takes twelve hours to harden.

Try to be accurate in gluing. Frequent re-gluing and bonding gives a messy finish, for the glue goes into lumps.

Removers

White spirit removes brown and clear adhesives; petrol lighter fuel removes rubber solution. Some brands of glue have their own remover. Nothing removes hardened resin once it has set.

To remove glue spots from leather, suede and fabric, let the glue dry, work it into a ball with your finger, and pick it off.

Storage and use

Always keep jars and tubes tightly closed.

When using rubber solution, pour small amounts into a saucer or bowl and replenish as needed.

With brown glues, soak paintbrush in white spirit between use.

Mix resin and hardener on an old tile or saucer. Wash immediately after use.

Top: velvet ribbon belt with ruched buckle framed in lace (see p 31 for instructions)
Middle: tie-dyed velvet softly gathered into a matching buckle
Bottom: velvet ribbon belt decorated with braid

Selection of turned belts using kid, calf, skiver, and Persian leather. The buckles are of various materials, including perspex, brass, painted enamel and leather. The top two lock into themselves, so are not adjustable.

Equipment

BASIC EQUIPMENT

A hard worktop at least 40″ (1 m) long. If necessary, use heavy cardboard or a strip of vinyl to protect the surface; newspaper dirties the materials.

Scissors   small and large pairs

Ruler or tape measure

Tailor's chalk and ballpoint pen for marking materials

Iron and ironing board

Hammer   two if possible, one for fabrics and skin only, the other for metals and hard objects

Sandpaper   medium grain, for scouring skins to hold glue

Wooden chopping board or flat piece of lead, needed only for large punches

An old tile on which to pare

A sewing machine is useful, but not essential. Most modern machines take a leather needle that stitches light leathers. Keep well-oiled if sewing over glue, but remember to wipe the foot before use. Do not force on heavy leathers.

TOOLS

Though not always used, a basic collection saves annoyance at small expense. See illustrations on p 18.

STORAGE AND CARE

Keep tools and equipment clean; white spirit removes old glue and dirt. When not in use, store tools in a drawer, box, or rack. Accessories store well in jam jars.

Always clean your worktop before starting work.

Never let your blades get blunt. Knives and scissors need kind treatment and regular sharpening or renewal.

Eyelet snapper, pliers, punch for large holes, rotary hole punch, needles, scissors for cutting heavy materials, scalpel

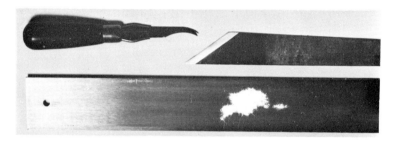

Tools for cutting leather: clicker's knife, paring knife, metal straight-edge rule. These are not essential, but they are quicker and more effective than scissors, ruler and scalpel.

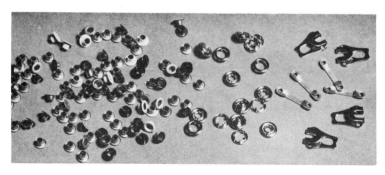

Accessories: eyelets, snaps, hooks and clasps

Working methods

I have given detailed notes on making four belts, which can be followed or used as a general guide. The turned belt (pp. 32–35) is perhaps the most useful, for it has countless variations. Elsewhere I have noted techniques that I hope will help, but it is more important that you develop your own methods to suit you and the materials you are working. There are no rules, only a few short cuts and suggestions.

FABRIC

Start with the heavier materials in a close weave: denim, wool, viyella, velvet, linen, felt. Avoid flimsy fabrics that stain easily with glue: silks, chiffon, satin, grosgrain, lawn. Patterned fabrics conceal mistakes more easily than plain ones, but be wary of those that need great accuracy, such as stripes.

The width of most dress fabrics is enough for one belt length, so buy only the depth you need.

First iron out the creases. Mark up the reverse side with tailor's chalk. Do not use ballpoint pen or pencil, because they show through when ironed. Cut with scissors; the clicker's knife is difficult to use except on very firm fabrics.

When gluing, wipe excess glue from the foam rubber and apply lightly with long strokes to wrong side. If you press too hard, the glue will soak through to the front. Use a clear adhesive on flimsy fabrics. Remember that glue takes longer to dry on fabric than on leathers.

LEATHER

When cutting with scissors, mark lines on the back of the skin with ballpoint or felt-tip pen. Try not to mark the front, even with tailor's chalk.

When cutting with a clicker's knife, weight the metal rule in position. Where needed, measure widths with a ruler at right-angles. Keep the right side of the skin face down.

Always cut strips from head to tail. Use the legs and belly for tags, buckles, buttons, decorative motifs, or other small pieces, provided the skin is not blemished. Use the skin thoughtfully to keep wastage to a minimum.

Apply glue with long, firm strokes. Glue the surface of shiny skins with brown glue, or sandpaper them to take rubber solution.

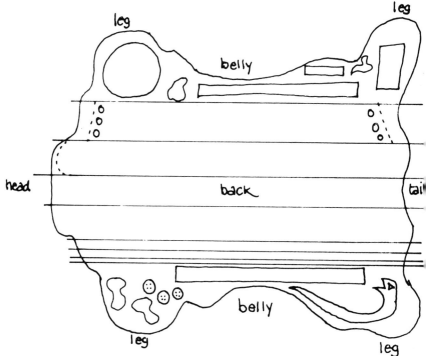

Sheepskin marked up for cutting. A whole skin is rarely used at once, so start a little way in from the belly, work over the back, and cut from the legs as needed. Always cut from head to tail.

Remember

Work with plenty of light.
Keep your worktop clean.
Keep your tools sharp and clean.
Remember that leather is supple, strong, and sensitive. Don't be

afraid to work it with your fingers, a hammer, or even water. You can stretch, gather, press, pull, or contract it. If pushed too far, it merely resists and very occasionally splits.

Joining leather

With small skins, you may need to join two strips. Pare down matching ends and glue, or stitch shapes together and incorporate them into the design.

Methods of joining leather

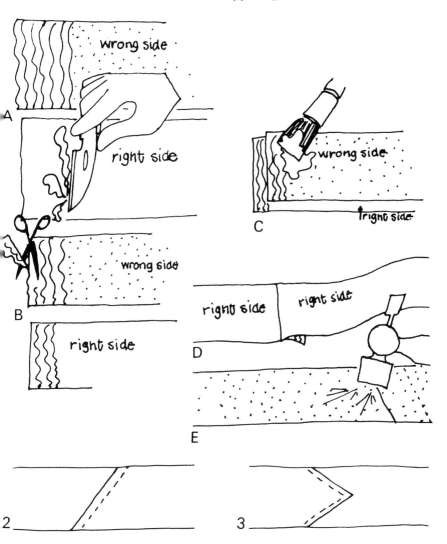

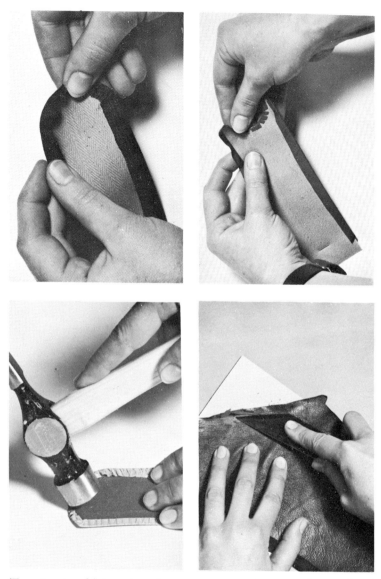

Top: turning fabric and suede onto convex and concave shapes. Good results depend on smooth edges, accurate gluing, and thin material.

Bottom, left: hammering down snakeskin on a curve and a sharp-angled corner; right, paring down leather; use a scalpel or paring knife on an old tile.

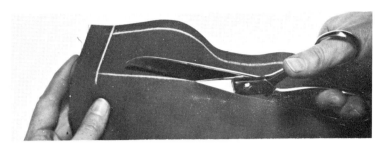

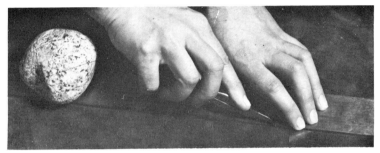

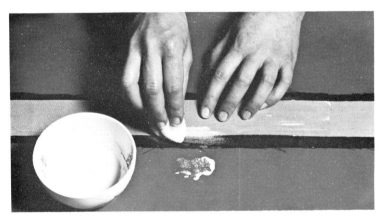

Top: cutting a strip of fabric for a turned belt

Middle: using the clicker's knife on leather. The left hand and a weight hold the metal rule in place. The cutting hand presses hard on the knife, drawing it smoothly along the metal straight-edge. It is possible to cut a strip $\frac{1}{8}''$ (3 mm) wide, but the method requires practice. Always cut on a piece of linoleum, vinyl, or heavy card, with the leather face down. For curved lines use the knife freehand or against a cardboard pattern, or mark with a pen and cut with scissors.

Bottom: covering a strip of lined fabric with rubber solution

23

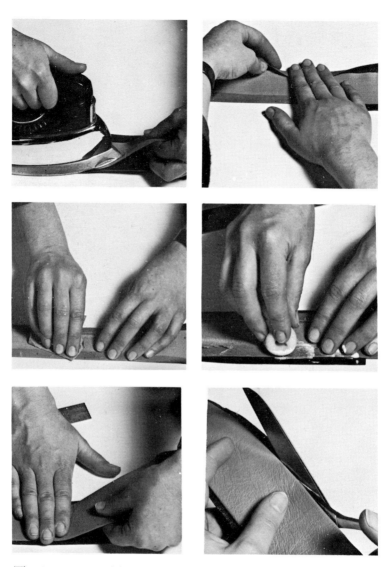

The importance of hands in a belt: 1 Ironing the interlining onto the reverse side of a leather strip; note the left hand. 2 Turning leather; the left hand presses it against the side of the lining, the right hand flattens it; note that only the border is glued. 3 Sandpapering leather. 4 Gluing the back of a turned belt, which is protected by a strip of skiver. 5 Sticking the two strips together. 6 Trimming, with the scissors at an angle.

Ribbon belts

*Working sample: olive velvet ribbon belt with braid buckle,
$1\frac{1}{2}''$ (4 cm) wide, backed with matching ribbon*

MATERIALS

2 yds (1.8 m) velvet ribbon, $1\frac{1}{2}''$ (4 cm) wide
1 yd (92 cm) flat braid, about $\frac{3}{8}''$ (1 cm) wide
1 yd (92 cm) adhesive interlining, $1\frac{1}{2}''$ (4 cm) wide
1 circular buckle with $1\frac{1}{2}''$ (4 cm) bar, in light metal, preferably
without prong
Sewing needle and thread to match braid and velvet
Rubber solution and foam rubber
Brown glue and paint brush (see pp 15–16)
Tape measure
Sewing machine (optional)

If possible, buy velvet ribbon that is $\frac{1}{8}''$ (3 mm) narrower than
the bar of the buckle. This is not difficult, for ribbon is often
slightly less than the stated width.

COLOUR SUGGESTIONS

Black velvet, black braid
Maroon velvet, dark pink braid

Turquoise velvet, sea green braid
Chocolate velvet, mid-brown braid
Rust velvet, orange braid
Try to match the interlining colour with the velvet.

TO COVER THE BUCKLE

Remove the prong with a pair of pliers. Paint both sides of the buckle and part of the bar with brown glue, and leave to dry for a few minutes. Then, starting at the back, wind the braid right side up round the buckle, as though you were bandaging a finger. Pull braid tight as you wind and do not overlap edges unnecessarily. When you reach the middle bar, make sure it is covered at either end by at least $\frac{1}{4}''$ (6 mm) of braid, so that when the belt passes through, no uncovered part may be seen. On completing the circle, cut off braid, turn in, and stitch to the back of the buckle.

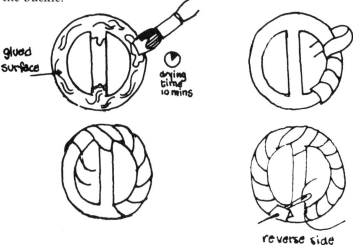

glued surface

drying time 10 mins

reverse side

MAKING THE BELT

Measure your waist over your clothes. Cut adhesive interlining and velvet ribbon as shown below.

Remember, the interlining should be slightly narrower than the velvet ribbon. If necessary, trim with scissors or clicker's knife.

interlining = waist + 4"/10 cm

velvet ribbon = waist x 2 + 10"/25 cm

26

Leaving 2″ (5 cm) of the velvet bare at one end, iron the inter-lining (or glue it if it is non-adhesive) to the wrong side of the velvet. Do not press too hard, for this will crush the velvet pile. Make sure the tape does not overlap the ribbon's edges.

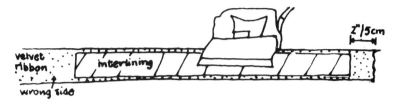

Spread rubber solution over the entire back (see pp 19 and 23). Be careful to go to, but not over, the edges. Leave to dry for several minutes, then press the ribbon back onto itself, covering the interlining. If the ribbon bubbles, pull up and replace.

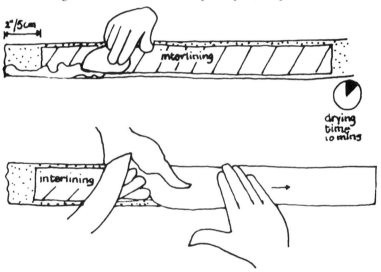

Squeeze the edges to ensure that they are properly stuck. Rein-force with machine or hand stitching, if you wish.

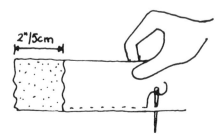

ATTACHING THE BUCKLE

Turn in the raw end and thread through the buckle from behind.
Fold back and stick or stitch to belt.

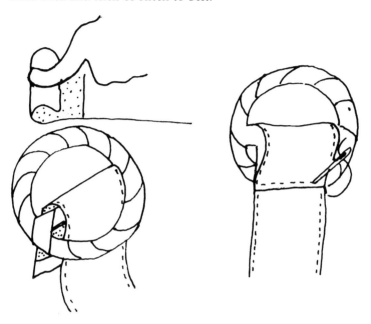

VARIATIONS

*Felt can be used like ribbon, as it does not fray. Above: silk
embroidered pincushion on a strip of felt, stitched for decoration and
to strengthen the belt. A hook and clasp adjust the length of the belt.*

Ribbon belts

Useful, but limited: petersham, heavy cotton, hessian (burlap) or even webbing for girths. Avoid flimsy materials such as satin and voile. Try to incorporate the ribbon into a specific design, otherwise it will look like ribbon, not a belt.

Home-made buckles

Contrast or emphasise the feeling of the belt with the buckle— sketch the ideas to see how they look.

To make your own buckle, glue together two pieces of stiff card. Mark out the shape you want and cut with scissors or scalpel (keep a blade specially for this because it is quickly blunted). Lids, tumblers and coins are good guides for curves. For square or oblong buckles, glue graph paper to the card and cut to shape. Cover with braid or ribbon.

To strengthen the buckle, glue a piece of very thin metal sheet between the two pieces of card.

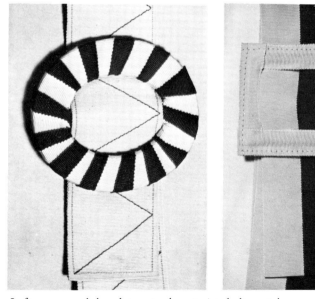

Left: cream and chocolate petersham twisted alternately round the buckle. The stitching on the belt reflects the geometric pattern. Right: striped belt in navy and lemon petersham. The square buckle was covered with strips of narrow ribbon and its outer edges machined.

Braid

Upholstery braid, dress trimming, and lampshade or curtain braid are good for decoration (see colour plate facing p 16) or for making the belt itself. But braid by itself looks like braid.

Top: open-work antique braid for the belt matched with modern tarnished braid on the buckle. Bottom, left: 'A Patrician Lady' by Bartholomeus de Bruyn, 1525 (Stadel Art Gallery, Frankfurt); right, braid and velvet belt in dull pinks and rust. The ribbon was stitched to the edge before a thin interlining was ironed on. A hook and eye hold the belt firm.

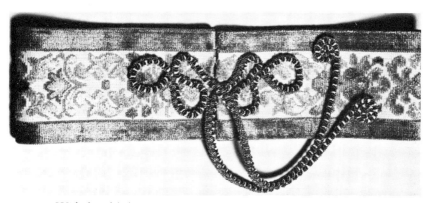

Wide braid belt in steel blue and dove grey. The raw ends were glued back on themselves; chair braid was glued and folded in half, then stitched to the belt to make a tie front. No lining was used, as the braid was heavy.

Ruched ribbon buckle .

See colour plate facing p 16, top. For this belt, the ribbon should be twice the width of the buckle's frame, and twice the length of the buckle's circumference. Hem the edges together at the back of the buckle, pulling the ribbon into a gathered tube. Fasten flowers, lace, feathers, to the back as wanted. Glue firmly to skiver, reverse sides together; trim the edges (see also p 43). Make the belt and attach the buckle as explained on pages 26–28.

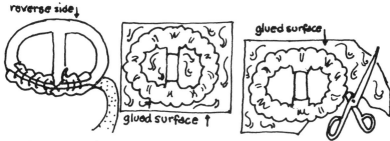

Storage and care

Hang belts in a cupboard, or coil them in a drawer. If velvet becomes creased, hold it over the steam of a kettle or leave it in the bathroom overnight. Iron gently, as with other materials. To clean, brush gently. Glued belts cannot be dry-cleaned.

Prongs, lengths of ribbon, bits of cardboard or braid may be useful for another belt, so keep them in a bag or box. Old bits of rubber solution are good for rubbing off dirt marks on belts.

Turned belts

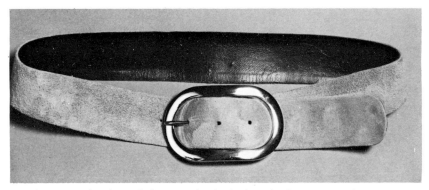

Working sample: beige belt in suede, backed with skiver, on a brass buckle, 1½″ (4 cm) wide

Materials

1 buckle with prong and 1½″ (4 cm) centre bar
Strip of suede, 2¼″ (6 cm) wide
Strip of skiver, 2″ (5 cm) wide
1¼ yds (1.1 m) adhesive interlining, 1½″ (4 cm) wide
Rubber solution glue and foam rubber (see p 16)
Rotary hole puncher
Scissors
Tape measure

COLOUR SUGGESTIONS

Olive, navy, tan, hunting green, black. Looks good with toning skiver.

LENGTH

Measure your waist or hips over clothes and add 7″ (18 cm); this allows a 4″ (10 cm) adjustment on the finished belt. Cut the interlining to this length and cut the suede strip and skiver strip 1″ (2.5 cm) longer. You may need to join the suede (see pp 20–21 for joining and cutting).

Left: turned leather belt with brass buckle and large eyelets. The decorative border is done with a bookbinding iron
Centre: horsebrass mounted on white patent
Right: raw-edge calf belt with antique brass buckle

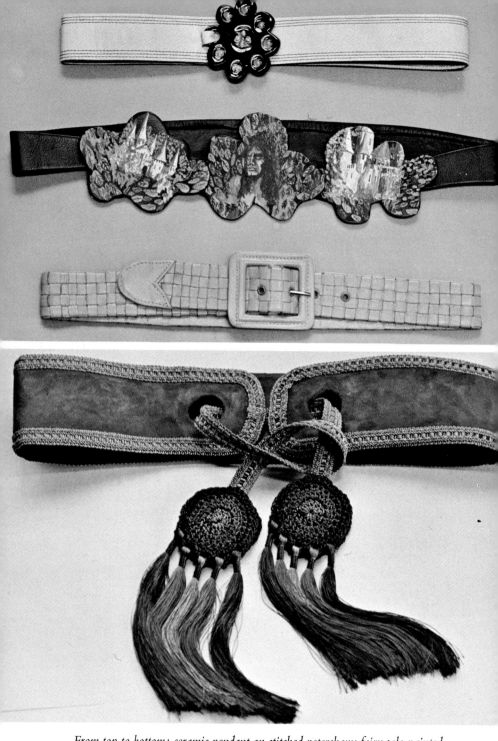

From top to bottom: ceramic pendant on stitched petersham; fairy tale painted on three interlocking leather discs; strips of leather woven into a belt, with

MAKING THE BELT

Make sure the interlining is $\frac{1}{8}''$ (3 mm) narrower than the bar of the buckle. Trim if necessary with scissors or clicker's knife. Round off one end, and taper the other. Iron (or glue if lining is non-adhesive) onto centre of suede strip, reverse sides together. Trim the suede at each end parallel to the lining.

Cover the outer edges with rubber solution. When dry, turn the edge of the suede onto the lining: start from the tapered end, work the suede up against the edge of the lining, fold over and press down. Always work towards yourself (see p 24).

Warning

Watch the glue. It is easy to splash and difficult to remove without leaving a mark. Be careful while turning the corner: work the suede round it with your thumb, and hammer down.

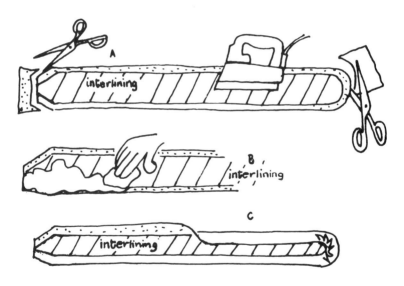

ATTACHING THE BUCKLE

Pare down the tapered end to prevent bulkiness. Mark and punch a slot centred 2″ (5 cm) from the end. (Use a slot punch, or make two holes side by side with the rotary puncher.) Thread the belt through the buckle from behind, fitting the prong through the slot. Fold back and glue to the belt.

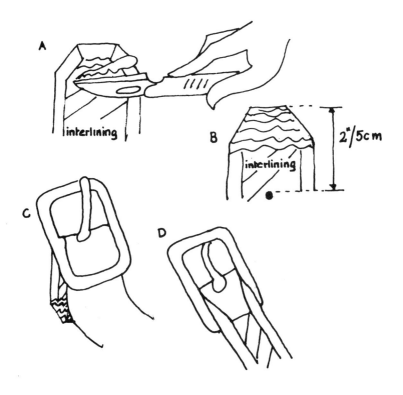

BACKING THE BELT

Place the belt on the skiver, both strips wrong side up. Cover the back of the belt with rubber solution, making sure the edges are well-coated; the skiver soaks up the excess. Lift the belt off, and coat the skiver with rubber solution.

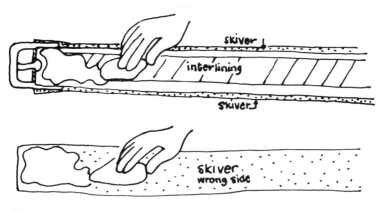

Stick the belt on the skiver, pressing into place. Make sure the skiver stays flat; if it crinkles, pull up the belt, adjust the skiver, and press the belt back again.

Turn the belt face down and rub along the back to smooth out small creases and to ensure the skiver is firmly stuck. Turn the belt the right side up again and trim it with scissors, keeping them tilted away from you to give a neat edge.

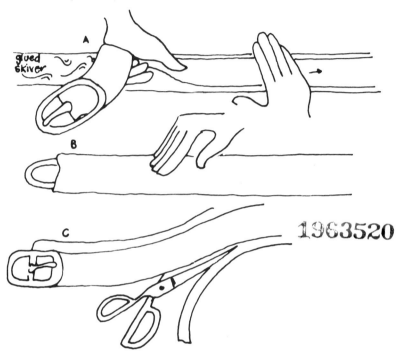

FINISHING THE BELT

Rub your fingers along the edges to remove any bits of glue. Measure, mark and punch five holes on the wrong side of the belt: 3″ (7.5 cm) from the end, 1″ (2.5 cm) apart, and centred from the edges. Make sure the prong fits the holes—no eyelets are needed for suede. Buff the suede side with a soft clothes brush.

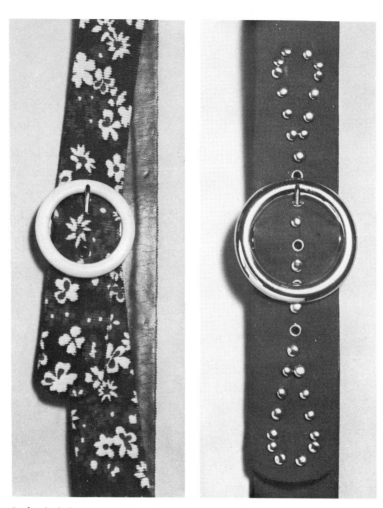

Left: dark brown needlecord printed with yellow and rust flowers. The bone buckle was dyed deep yellow. Before inserting the eyelets, mark the position on the back of the belt and punch with rotary hole puncher. Always use eyelets on fabric belts to prevent fraying.

Right: here the eyelets form a pattern with brass studs on a dark green belt. The pattern was planned and marked out on the back of the lining, the holes punched, and the studs put in before the backing was stuck on. The eyelets were then inserted where planned. Remember always to cut the strip of material 1″ (2.5 cm) wider than the lining.

Buckles

There is a wide choice of modern buckles, but mostly they are lightweight and undecorated. It is worth searching for something different—antique buckles, foreign buckles, theatrical costume buckles. At little cost I have found beautiful ones in enamel, silver, brass, French paste, and copper. Some were delicate, or intricate; some, heavy and simple. Each seemed to dictate the material I should use. Remember to cut the interlining $\frac{1}{8}''$ (3 mm) narrower than the bar.

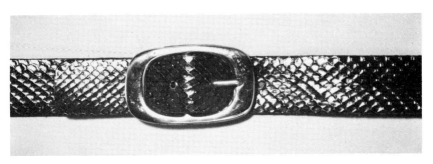

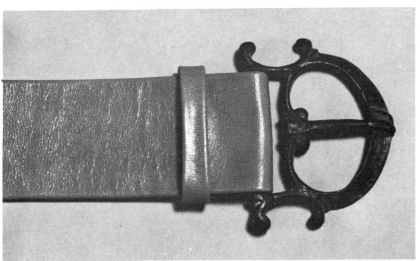

Top: the texture of the watersnake heightens the simplicity of the brass buckle. The skin turned onto the lining was sandpapered to hold the glue and backing.

Bottom: this delicately ornate buckle seemed to demand the richness of a finely grained kid. A very thin skin was used.

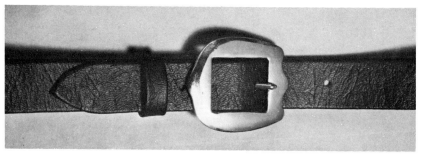

Above, top: metal and enamel buckle in gold and maroon. The texture of the wool belt reflects the chased pattern of the metal.

Above: heavy brass buckle with black plastic belt. The skiver backing was stuck with brown glue, as plastic is difficult to sandpaper. The loop was made from a turned strip held with an eyelet.

Below: brass square with interlocking centrepiece patterned with resin (design: Olga Solomon). The belt turns back on itself with poppers for adjustment. The turned edges of leather were sandpapered before machining; this should always be done.

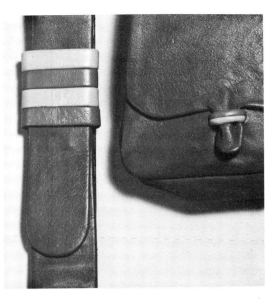

Left: old watch-face sunk into clear perspex, bought as a paper-weight and now mounted on tan patent. If patent is stiff to work, warm it in front of a fire. Hooks and eyelets fasten the belt behind.

Right: plain leather belt with striped fastening to match a bag. Turn four strips, back with skiver, and attach as a loop to one end of belt.

Tooling

Usually for bookbinding, but may be adapted to belts (see colour plate facing p 32, left).

Always damp both sides of the leather with vinegar or water. Stamping tools may be used cold with a hammer, but wheels for continuous patterns are best heated (try on a remnant first).

Borders are best done once the belt is made, but free patterns may be done before. Work on a smooth, hard surface.

Storage and care

Brush fabric and suede with a clothes brush when finished, and wipe leather with a cloth. Hang by the buckle in a cupboard, or coil in a drawer, keeping the grain side out to prevent creasing. Clean suede lightly with a wire brush or a ball of dry rubber solution. For grease marks, cover very lightly with talcum powder and rub in gently. Polish leather, or iron at a very low heat.

Wide belts, covered buckles

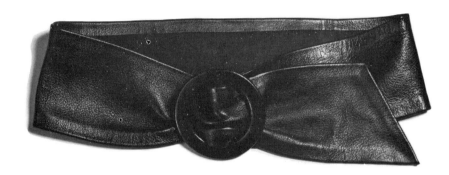

Working sample: Persian leather soft belt, $3\frac{1}{4}''$ (8.3 cm) wide, in navy. The buckle is covered with leather taken from the same skin.

MATERIALS

Strip of leather $4\frac{1}{4}''$ (11 cm) wide
Square of leather, $4'' \times 4''$ (10 × 10 cm), must be very thin and supple
Square of skiver, $4'' \times 4''$ (10 × 10 cm)
1 circular buckle, $2''$ (5 cm) bar, without prong
Rubber solution and foam rubber
Brown petroleum mixture and paint brush
Small scissors
Scalpel or paring knife
Ruler and tape measure

COLOUR SUGGESTIONS

Red, emerald, navy, black, chocolate. Works well in both leather and suede. Try to match or tone the skiver.

LENGTH

Measure your waist over your clothes and add $7\frac{1}{2}''$ (19 cm). Cut the strip of leather to this length; you may need to join two strips (p 21).

MAKING THE BELT

With the grain down, trim the left end of the leather strip at a downward angle. Square off the other end.

Remember that a belt fastens to the left for a woman and to the right for a man, so trim your end accordingly. To check, wrap the strip round your waist as though it were the finished belt.

On the back, draw a line $\frac{1}{2}''$ (1.3 cm) from the edge. Carefully glue a strip $1''$ (2.5 cm) wide round the edge, using rubber solution. To make it easier, use a metal rule or a piece of brown paper as a guide. Leave to dry.

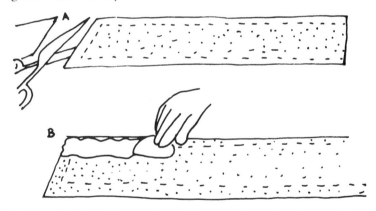

Fold the leather like a piece of paper along the line, and press down. Start from the squared end, work round the belt, but leave the corners unturned. Do not turn the squared end.

Warning

Avoid a wavy edge. Keep the leather taut while you are turning.

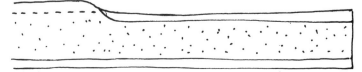

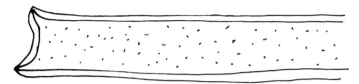

SHARP-ANGLED CORNERS

Squeeze the 'ear' into a flat triangle and cut off towards the centre of the belt. Do not cut too near the outer edge. Hammer down.

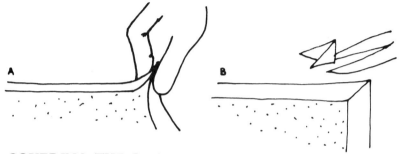

COVERING THE BUCKLE

Always choose a very thin leather, either to match or contrast with the belt. Snakeskin is excellent for this sort of work, or supple leather or suede. If you can find nothing thin enough, hammer the leather to greater suppleness. Alternatively, take the leather square and pare down the flesh with a scalpel or paring knife. Work slowly, removing the flesh in paper thin layers. Practice helps, and a sharp blade is essential. This method is not always satisfactory, for it is easy to.make holes and any unevenness will show on the front.

Paint the back of the leather square with brown adhesive, press the buckle face down in the middle, and coat the back with brown adhesive. Leave to dry.

Trim leather to within $\frac{1}{2}''$ (1.3 cm) of the buckle. With small scissors, cut out the middle sections, $\frac{1}{2}''$ (1.3 cm) from the curved rim and $\frac{3}{8}''$ (1 cm) from the centre bar. Nick the inside curved edges.

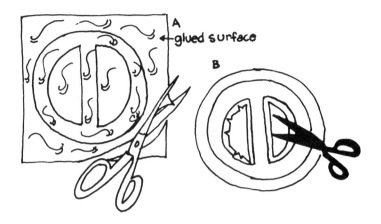

Using the side of your thumb, work the leather up against the side of the buckle. Then, with the tip of your thumb, press it down on the back. Remember that leather is supple, so stretch and compress it as much as you want, to mould it round the curve, but do this before it touches the buckle: once it has stuck, you can do little with it except rip it up and start again.

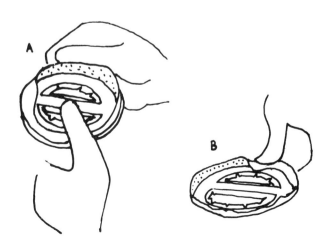

Turn the inside edges of the buckle. This is difficult, so practise first with fabric or leather on a piece of stiff card.

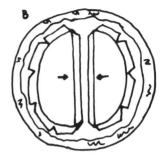

Hammer the back with inward strokes, sandpaper lightly, and coat with brown adhesive. Glue the square of skiver and press the buckle onto it, wrong sides together. Rub the skiver hard to make sure it is properly stuck. Trim the outside edge of the buckle, keeping the scissors tilted away from you.

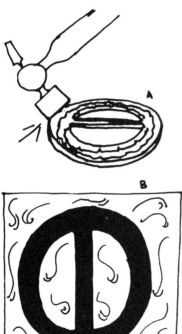

Turn the buckle over and trim the inside edges, using your index finger behind to guide the point of the scissors.

Rub down the raw edges of the skiver.

ATTACHING THE BUCKLE

Pare down the wrong side of the squared end of the belt. Trim, and sandpaper the turned leather for 3" (7.5 cm). Thread the belt through the buckle, gathering it to fit the centre bar. Fold back and glue down.

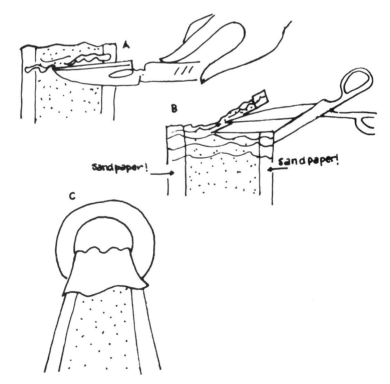

STORAGE AND CARE

Roll the belt, grain side out, or hang it from the buckle in a cupboard. Polish out scratches; iron out creases with low heat.

VARIATIONS

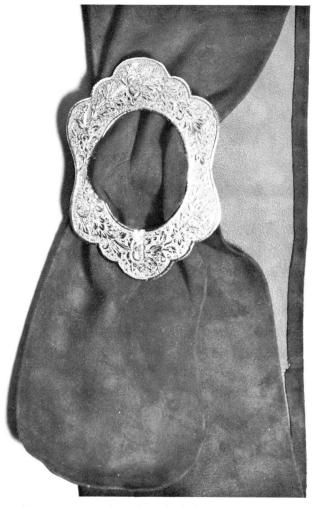

Softly gathered cayenne-coloured suede belt with deep rounded end. The silver buckle is Persian, embossed with flowers in traditional style. The prong has been left off deliberately. Soft colours seem to suit this style—smoky blue, gold, old rose pink.

Duck-egg blue suede embroidered with dark silk on a plain buckle covered with matching suede. The belt was machined and turned, then backed with skiver to hide loose ends. This could also be done on fabric, though flimsy material would need to be lined or machined double.

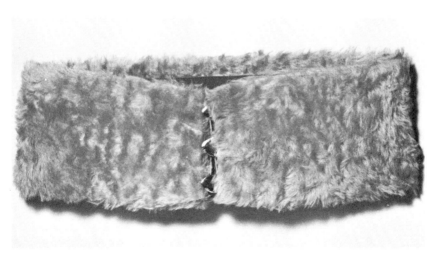

'Fur' fabric, backed with 3″ (7.5 cm) wide adhesive tape to prevent the edges fraying. The brass clasp makes the belt non-adjustable.

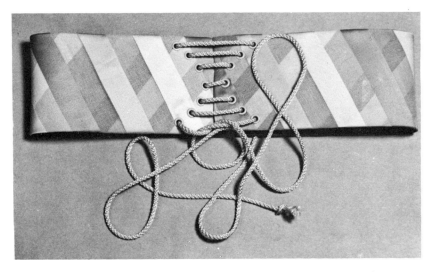

Above: voile striped with satin in pale greens and yellows, laced with yellow cord. Two layers of fabric were used to make the criss-cross pattern; the strips were stitched together, then ironed and turned onto green interlining, and backed with green skiver.

Below: wide leather belt in purple, knotted together with raw-edge thongs cut from the same skin. The lining was cut to shape, the leather turned onto it, the thonging threaded and knotted through round buttons, then glued to the back of each point. Flat buttons were sewn on for decoration and to secure the thonging further.

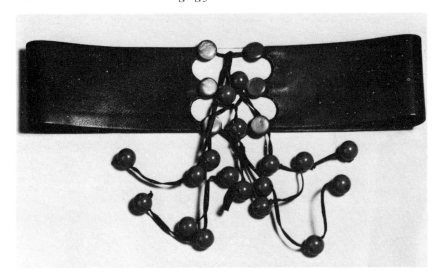

Thonging

Cut strips of leather and suede $\frac{1}{2}''$ (1.3 cm) wide; join where necessary to make required length. Glue the back with rubber solution; fold edges simultaneously to meet in the centre. Hammer down.

The strips may also be used raw-edge, but if the skin is not dyed right through, the edges will show white.

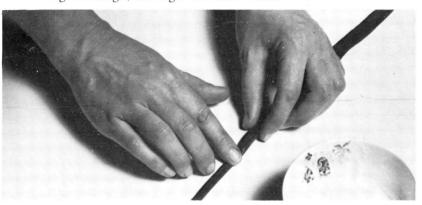

COVERED BUTTONS

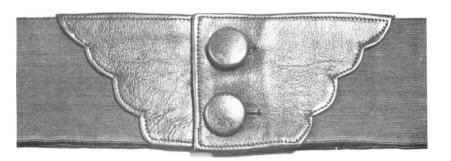

Wide elastic belt with buttoned leather frontispiece in dark green. The front was cut from interlining, covered with leather and glued to the elastic. The buttons were covered and sewn on; the buttonholes were cut; skiver was cut to the shape of the front and glued on at the back; the edges were machined. Remember to work out which way the buttons should go. Elastic can be dyed in a saucepan.

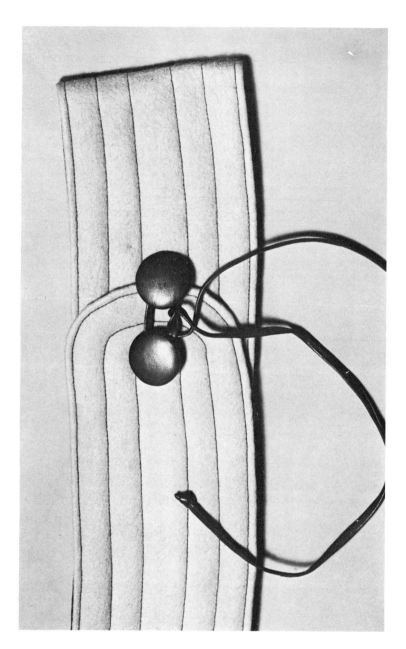

Felt cummerbund lined and backed, with leather button fastening. A very thin strip of foam was glued to the lining under the felt to bring the machined stripes into relief. The thonging is fastened to the back of the belt through a slit.

To cover a button

The principles are the same as for covering a buckle (pp 42–45). Choose metal, bone, or wooden buttons with a smooth surface; glue to fabric or pared leather, trim the edges and turn onto the back and finish with skiver.

The thinner the material, the better the result. Always use brown adhesive, apply carefully, and make sure it is dry to the touch before bonding. Take special care on flimsy fabrics.

Decoration

Vary your buttons with shapes embroidered on fabric or machined on leather before the button is covered, or use acrylic paint, textures of snakeskin or striped fabric, brass studs.

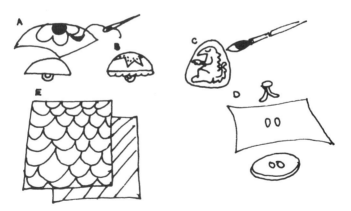

More ideas

Raw-edge kid leather backed with cheap sheepskin and stitched. The ends fold back through loops to allow adjustment. The brass buckle was cast by a local foundry from a prototype: the centre part was a metal disc stuck with mosaic squares, and the half circles were cut from plastic rings. Plaster of paris is usually best for modelling.

RAW EDGES

Leather that is too stiff to turn neatly can be used raw-edge and looks good with heavy buckles (see colour plate facing p 32, right).

Cut with a clicker's knife and metal straight edge; it is vital to get a strip with clean, straight edges. Pare down one end, punch a slot for the prong and thread over the buckle. A backing of skiver or cheap leather can be glued or stitched. For thick backing, cut with a clicker's knife to the same width as the belt.

If the edges are pale because the leather is not dyed right through, colour with dye, polish, or wax.

For large prongs, use a drive punch for the holes. If the leather is weak, use the large 'sale' eyelets and washers (colour plate facing p 32, left). Work on lead or wood.

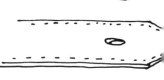

HAND STITCHING

If machine stitching is difficult, hand stitch heavy leather. You will need a stitch gauge, an awl, a leather needle and waxed cotton thread or buttonhole twist.

Mark out the line of stitching with the gauge and puncture the holes with the awl. In some cases it is possible to make holes with the unthreaded leather needle of a sewing machine.

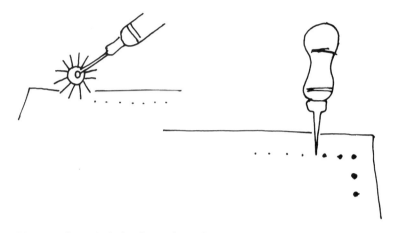

Use running stitch, back stitch or, for greater strength, the cobbler's stitch. Glue loose ends between belt strip and backing.

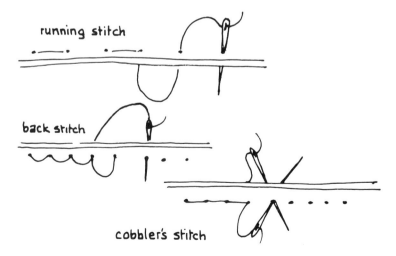

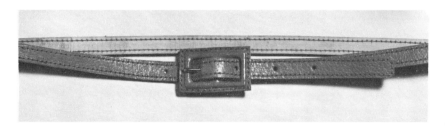

Above, top: Tan pigskin belt, raw-edge, with raw-edge buckle. Remove the prong before covering a buckle; replace it with pliers when finished.

Above: lichen green kid belt, hand stitched with cream silk. The buckle is made with two layers of cardboard; the belt is turned, stitched, and attached with the loop to the buckle. Remember to leave space between the stitches for punching eyelet holes.

Below: two striped elastic belts with buckled leather frontispiece. The first is stitched raw-edge; the second, turned and stitched.

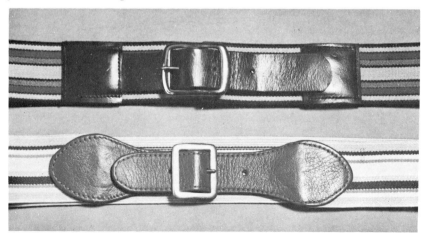

Above: plaited cord belt in scarlet and black, tied with two pairs of tassels. It was made from two uncut lengths, 4 yds (3.6 m) each, which were folded into three with 14″ (35 cm) left at either end.

Below: strips of leather knotted into a belt, with a leather tab fastening, in pale blue and navy. The knot is a clove hitch; try macramé for other ideas.

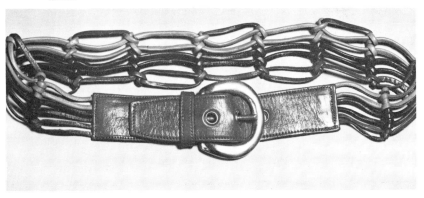

HEAVY CORD

Good for knotting, plaiting, tying. Wrap sticky tape round cord at cutting point to prevent it untwisting, but glue or stitch raw ends when finishing off. Try sailing rope, nylon cord, or make lengths from leather (colour plate, facing p 17). String and cord can also be covered with very thin materials.

NEEDLEWORK

Techniques include embroidery, tapestry, knitting, crochet, done either by hand or machine. Mainly for decoration, with exciting materials: silk, raffia, sequins, beads, string, wool, shoe laces. Make tassels, bobbles, braids; crochet pouches to hang from the waist; knit a twenty-foot (six-metre) belt.

Above, top: emerald suede belt with buckle in scarlet, lemon and emerald. The tapestry end increases the mood with similar colours and pattern.

Above: sequin motif mounted on black velvet (worked by Lilian Warton). The belt is curved and fastens with hooks and eyelets.

DYEING AND PRINTING

Try dyeing threads, elastic, chamois suede; tie-and-dye fabric for a belt or bag; or dye the surface of leather to match a dress or shoes.

Use hot or cold dyes; the instructions are on the pack for chemical dyes you buy. Experiment with natural dyes from nettles, blackberries, onion skins.

SHAPED BELTS

These need practice, as curves are difficult to turn.

Always use firm interlining; mark out the pattern on the back with a ballpoint pen, preferably using a hard shape to guide you. Cut carefully with scissors—the quality of the belt depends on the cleanness of the pattern.

Iron the shaped interlining onto material, glue, turn, and back. See p 22 for working methods, and colour plate facing p 33, top middle for example.

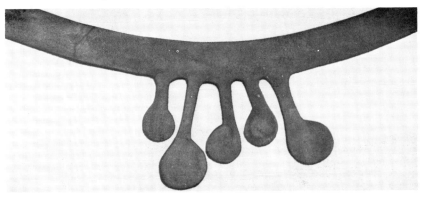

Decorative choker: globules in grey suede turned onto a curved band, made like a miniature belt. It fastens with a popper.

UNORTHODOX MATERIALS

Keep your eyes open! Adapt a horsebrass (colour plate facing p 32, centre), or a bunch of keys, nuts, bolts, stones, pebbles, bottle tops, even a flat wooden butter dish.

SOURCES OF INSPIRATION

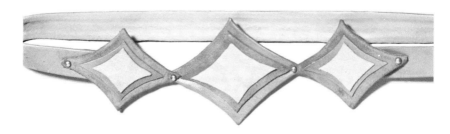

Above, top: the cloisters of St Triomphine, Arles, France.

Above: suede and leather belt in yellow and dark orange gives a similar effect of shade and light between curved lines.

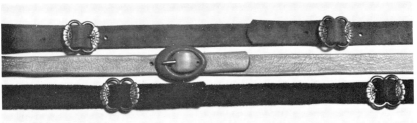

Above, top: detail from 'The Tailor' by Giovan Battista Moroni, about 1571. (Reproduced by courtesy of the Trustees, The National Gallery, London)

Above: three narrow belts, turned to centre as in thonging. The suede belts have antique silver buckles; the leather belt is in bright yellow, green and turquoise. Narrow leather strips are also used in a scarlet belt on the colour plate facing page 17.

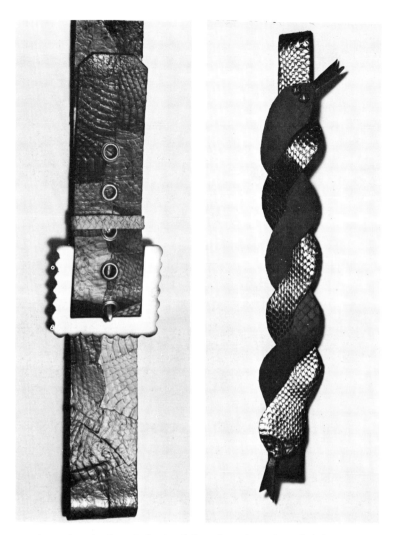

Snake and snakeskin. Left: brightly coloured patchwork belt in water-snake. The pieces were stuck on at random, trimmed ¼″ (1 cm) from the lining, and turned. The surface was then coated with clear acrylic varnish.

Right: intertwining snake in green watersnake and sueded python. The two skins are joined at the back on the straight. The shaped front is strengthened with very thin metal.

Perspex

There are limited suppliers of perspex, but some dealers will cut it to your design.

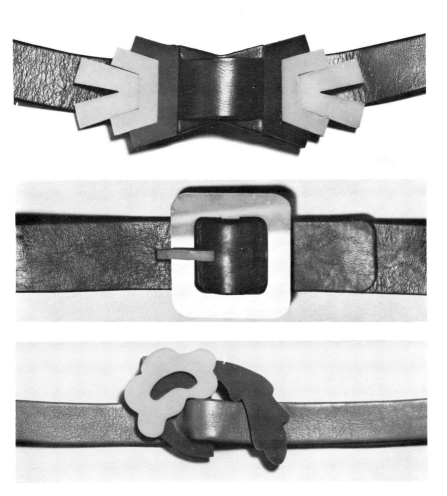

Top: navy, turquoise and yellow perspex sections mounted on a frame covered with navy leather.

Middle: deep yellow perspex buckle with giant prong on tan leather. The holes were made with an oblong drive punch.

Bottom: yellow flower glued to a leaf, which is also the bar for the belt. Use special adhesive prepared for perspex.

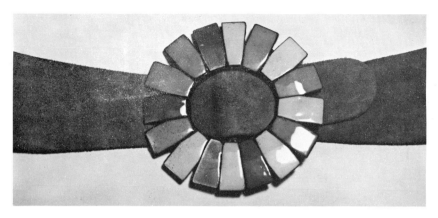

Left, top: sunburst in yellows, oranges and reds. Each 'ray' was cut out and enamelled separately, then glued to an oval buckle that had been covered with skiver.

Middle: maybug in pinks and maroon. Copper wire defines the colour areas. Mounted on card and backed with skiver.

Bottom: interlocking arabesque buckle in rust and cinnamon colours. The copper wire boldly announces the pattern.

Enamelling is possible in a very small kiln, and introduces a range of colours and textures to contrast with the belt.

Linked segments. Top: squares of copper enamelled with daisies on dark green, joined by copper wire.

Below: brass discs painted with acrylic; the path, windows and rim were left unpainted.

The boldness and fluency of the two designs seem to demand simple, straight belts. They fold round brass bars that were glued to the back of the outer discs with a resin adhesive.

The Arabesque enamel is by Romayne Pike, Castle Fantasia by Craig Baber, and other enamelled buckles by Liz Purchas.

Index

adhesives, 15–6, 19, 20, 61
adhesive tape, 14–5, 47
backing, 10, 13, 14, 15, 34–5
blades, 17, 29, 42
braid, 25, 26, 29, 30, 31
buckles, 13, 20, 25–6, 28, 29, 31, 33–4, 36–8, 40, 42–5
buttons, 20, 48, 49, 50, 51
calfskin, 11, 12
cardboard, 17, 23, 29, 54
corners, 22, 33, 42
cowhide, 12
curves, 22, 23, 29, 57
cutting, 18, 19–20, 23, 27
design, 1, 21, 29, 38, 61, 63
Domestic leather, 11
dyeing, 36, 49, 52, 57
embroidery, 28, 47, 51, 56
eyelets, 18, 35, 36, 38, 39, 52
eyelet snapper, 18
fabric, 10, 13, 16, 19, 23, 36, 47, 48
felt, 10, 19, 28, 50
foam rubber, 15, 16, 19, 50
gluing, 15–6, 19, 20, 22, 23, 24
goatskin, 11–2
grain, 11, 12, 37, 39
greasemarks, 39
hammer, 17, 21, 22, 44
hides, 12
hooks, 18, 28, 30, 39
interlining, 10, 13, 15, 24, 26, 27, 30, 32, 37
ironing, 11, 17, 19, 24, 27, 33, 57
joining, 21, 22, 32
kid, 11, 37, 52, 54
knives, 17

clicker's, 18, 19, 20, 52
paring, 18, 22, 42
leather, 7, 8, 9, 11–2, 14, 16, 18, 19–21, 22, 23, 24
imitation, 13, 38
cleaning, 16, 39
loop, 38, 39
materials, 7, 9, 10–5, 17, 19, 37, 47
metal, 7, 13, 16, 18, 37, 38
sheet, 29, 60
paring, 21, 22, 33, 42, 45
patent, 11, 16, 39
Persian leather, 11, 40
Petersham, 15, 29
pigskin, 11, 12, 54
plastics, 13, 14, 16, 38
punches, 18, 33, 35, 52, 61
raw-edges, 10, 12, 13, 14, 15, 49, 52, 54
ribbon, 25, 26, 27, 28, 29
sandpaper, 16, 17, 20, 24, 38
sheepskin, 11, 12, 20, 52
skiver, 14, 24, 34–5, 38
snakeskins, 12–3, 16, 22, 37, 51, 60
stitching, 10, 12, 17, 21, 27, 28, 48, 53, 54
storage, 13, 16, 17, 31, 39, 46
suede, 9, 11–3, 16, 22, 32, 33, 35, 39, 46, 47, 58
thonging, 48, 49, 50, 59
tools, 17–8, 20
trimming, 24, 26, 33
turned belts, 10, 11, 12, 13, 14–5, 19, 22, 23, 24, 32–9
working methods, 19–24
worktop, 17, 20